ALTERNATOR
BOOKS™

MICHELLE OBAMA

POLITICAL ICON

HEATHER E. SCHWARTZ

Lerner Publications ◆ Minneapolis

Lerner Publications Company
An imprint of Lerner Publishing Group, Inc.
241 First Avenue North
Minneapolis, MN 55401 USA

For reading levels and more information, look up this title at www.lernerbooks.com.

Main body text set in Aptifer Sans LT Pro.
Typeface provided by Linotype AG.

Editor: Alison Lorenz **Designer:** Lindsey Owens

Library of Congress Cataloging-in-Publication Data

Names: Schwartz, Heather E., author.
Title: Michelle Obama : political icon / Heather E. Schwartz.
Description: Minneapolis : Lerner Publications, [2021] | Series: Boss Lady Bios
   (Alternator books) | Includes bibliographical references and index. | Audience:
   Ages 8–12. | Audience: Grades 4–6. | Summary: "Former First Lady Michelle
   Obama is a lawyer, a best-selling author, and a powerful advocate for equal
   rights. From Chicago to Harvard, the White House and beyond, follow Obama's
   trailblazing and inspiring journey"— Provided by publisher.
Identifiers: LCCN 2019036710 (print) | LCCN 2019036711 (ebook) |
   ISBN 9781541597075 (lib. bdg.) | ISBN 9781541599703 (ebook)
Subjects: LCSH: Obama, Michelle, 1964– —Juvenile literature. | Presidents'
   spouses—United States—Biography—Juvenile literature. | African American
   women—Biography—Juvenile literature. | Lawyers—Illinois—Chicago—
   Biography—Juvenile literature. | African American women lawyers—Illinois—
   Chicago—Biography—Juvenile literature. | Chicago (Ill.)—Biography—Juvenile
   literature.
Classification: LCC E909.O24 S39 2021 (print) | LCC E909.O24 (ebook) |
   DDC 973.932092 [B]—dc23

LC record available at https://lccn.loc.gov/2019036710
LC ebook record available at https://lccn.loc.gov/2019036711

Manufactured in the United States of America
1-47811-48251-10/22/2019

TABLE OF CONTENTS

Michelle Obama addresses the Democratic National Convention in 2008.

TAKING THE STAGE

MICHELLE OBAMA HAD WORKED HARD, CAREFULLY CRAFTING HER MESSAGE. She'd practiced her speech over and over. On August 25, 2008, her brother, Craig, introduced her to the vast audience of the Democratic National Convention. About twenty thousand people sat crowded inside the Pepsi Center in Denver, Colorado, waiting to hear her words. Thousands more watched on their TV sets at home.

Obama strode across the stage, stepped up to the microphone, and began to speak. Her speech was in support of her husband, Barack, who was running for president. But it was also an opportunity to speak for herself.

"It was a big moment, for sure. . . . But the truth is . . . it was also strangely kind of a small moment," she wrote later. "Stages, audiences, lights, applause. These were becoming more normal than I'd ever thought they could be."

Obama was already growing into the role she would soon claim: First Lady of the United States of America.

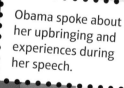

Obama spoke about her upbringing and experiences during her speech.

The South Side of Chicago in the 1960s

CHAPTER 1

CITY GIRL

BORN ON JANUARY 17, 1964, MICHELLE LAVAUGHN ROBINSON GREW UP ON THE SOUTH SIDE OF CHICAGO. Her father, Fraser Robinson III, was a city worker. Her mother, Marian Robinson, stayed home to raise Michelle and her older brother, Craig. Michelle was always motivated to succeed in life, and her close-knit family supported her goals and dreams.

Obama has always been close with her brother. Sometimes people even think they're twins!

Michelle was smart and ambitious. But she faced challenges too. Her family didn't have a lot of money. Her father had multiple sclerosis, a disease that made it difficult for him to walk. Many people in her neighborhood struggled with low incomes.

But Michelle wasn't shy about taking charge and going for what she wanted. As a four-year-old, she insisted on learning to play the piano. She challenged her teacher's methods by learning advanced songs on her own. In kindergarten, she felt so bad about a spelling mistake that she made sure she got it right the next day.

Michelle learned from an early age that her family valued education.

GETTING IT DONE!

When Michelle made a mistake in school, she would go home and study hard. The next day, she asked to try again.

Her parents expected her to get good grades. But speaking and writing in the way her teachers taught her sometimes made Michelle feel different from her peers. At the age of ten, Michelle was hanging out with some cousins when one of them asked, "How come you talk like a white girl?"

Michelle was embarrassed. "It was hard to know what to do," she wrote later. "Everyone seemed to fit in, except for me."

Still passionate about education, Obama sometimes speaks at graduation ceremonies.

YOU'RE THE BOSS

Everyone makes mistakes, and everyone can learn from them. If you get a bad grade or fail a test in school, do all you can to turn things around. Learn the correct answers, and study so you don't forget. Rewrite an essay to include any information you might have missed.

Once you've done your work, you'll be in a better position to ask to take a test again or turn in a new essay. Your teacher may be willing to give you a second chance if you can prove you know your stuff. Even if you don't get a do-over, turn in any extra work you've done. You'll know you tried your hardest!

Obama visits with students at Whitney M. Young Magnet High School.

CHAPTER 2
RISING STAR

WHEN MICHELLE WAS IN FIFTH GRADE, HER SCHOOL DEVELOPED SPECIAL EXTRA ACTIVITIES FOR GIFTED AND TALENTED STUDENTS. The group did such activities as attend a community college writing class and dissect a rat. Michelle loved the program and worked hard to be the best.

After eighth grade, Michelle went to Whitney M. Young Magnet High School. There, Michelle learned alongside other exceptional students. She worked hard, did well, and started to feel confident. "At Whitney Young, it was safe to be smart . . . you never hid your intelligence for fear of someone saying you talked like a white girl," she wrote later.

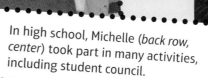

In high school, Michelle (*back row, center*) took part in many activities, including student council.

Obama and her brother, Craig

Michelle's brother, Craig, was at Princeton University, and she wanted to go there too. She was surprised when a college counselor at school told her she shouldn't try to apply. But she wasn't discouraged. Instead, she decided to prove her doubter wrong.

"I WASN'T GOING TO LET ONE PERSON'S OPINION DISLODGE EVERYTHING I THOUGHT I KNEW ABOUT MYSELF."

Michelle got an assistant principal to write her a recommendation letter. She focused her application essay on her family and her experiences. Soon her dream school accepted her.

At Princeton, most of the other students were white men. Michelle formed strong friendships with other black students. She was aware that Princeton was a privileged world very different from where she grew up.

Princeton University

After Princeton, she went to Harvard Law School. Then she got a job at a law firm. She earned a high salary and had her own assistant working for her. Soon she agreed to mentor a summer associate. That associate was Barack Obama.

Obama received her law degree from Harvard in 1988.

Barack Obama

Obama impressed her right away. He was older than she was, but he'd taken time off to work before attending Harvard Law School. He was interesting and easy to talk to. She liked him a lot, but she didn't think of him as a potential boyfriend. She even tried to set him up with a friend.

CHAPTER 3
FIERCE FIRST LADY

The Obamas campaigned together during Barack's presidential run.

MICHELLE ROBINSON AND BARACK OBAMA GREW CLOSER, AND BEFORE THE SUMMER WAS OVER, THEIR RELATIONSHIP HAD TURNED ROMANTIC. His ambition inspired her. His drive to address racial issues in the United States helped her see that she didn't want to be a lawyer. She had to find a career she felt more passionate about. Meanwhile, she grew nervous that her devotion to Obama could derail her goals if she wasn't careful.

"I WAS DEEPLY, DELIGHTFULLY IN LOVE WITH A GUY WHOSE FORCEFUL INTELLECT AND AMBITION COULD POSSIBLY END UP SWALLOWING MINE. . . . I [NEEDED] TO QUICKLY ANCHOR MYSELF ON TWO FEET."

Robinson eventually found a job at Chicago's City Hall. It was very different from her work as a lawyer. She liked helping people improve their lives. In her next position, she founded the Chicago chapter of Public Allies, a program that prepares young people for jobs in public service. Robinson finally felt connected to her work. She knew she had found her new direction.

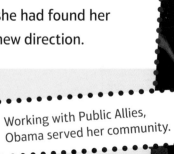

Working with Public Allies, Obama served her community.

Michelle Obama in 2007

Meanwhile, she was growing personally too. In 1992 she married Barack and became Michelle Obama. In 1998 they had their first daughter, Malia. By then Obama had a job at the University of Chicago. She'd always known about the college, having grown up in the city. But it had felt a world away from her life. In her position as associate dean of student services, she set out to change that.

GETTING IT DONE!

When she worked at the University of Chicago, Obama created a community service program. It brought college students, staff, and faculty together to work with people who lived in the area.

Juggling motherhood and a career wasn't easy. But Obama wanted to work. After her second daughter, Sasha, was born in 2001, she went back to work full-time at the University of Chicago Medical Center. The job's focus was community outreach, and Obama was excited to do the work she loved again.

Her husband worked in politics, and his jobs often kept him away from home. As a couple, the Obamas worked to create a stable, loving home for their family. Then, when her husband was elected to the US Senate, Obama discovered an even more privileged world than she had experienced at Princeton or Harvard. She was again surrounded by powerful people, mainly white men. She sensed that many in Washington saw her as Mrs. Obama, the senator's wife, rather than a successful woman in her own right.

Her husband's political career meant Obama's family was often in the spotlight.

Obama worked hard to make sure her daughters had a normal life.

It was an uncomfortable feeling that would soon become an even bigger issue in her life. Her husband wanted to run for president, and Obama was scared. She didn't know if she wanted that kind of life for herself or her children. But she also didn't want to stand in the way. Believing with all her heart that he could help the American people, she agreed.

Obama jumped into campaigning while continuing to care for her kids. In 2008 her husband was elected the forty-fourth president of the United States and the country's first African American president. Obama became the country's first African American First Lady. She was determined to use her power—and her own experiences—to do meaningful work for her country.

Barack Obama became president in 2009.

CHAPTER 4

THE WHITE HOUSE AND BEYOND

Obama helped children plant vegetables in her garden at the White House.

AS FIRST LADY, OBAMA DECIDED TO FOCUS ON HEALTH AND WELLNESS. In 2009 she planted a garden at the White House to inspire Americans to think about eating healthfully. Then, in 2010, she launched the Let's Move! campaign. Her goal was to fight childhood obesity and help children and families live healthful lives.

arn to play   ted Way

Obama played soccer with star player David Beckham (*right*) to encourage kids to exercise.

In 2011 Obama worked with Jill Biden, Vice President Joe Biden's wife, to launch Joining Forces. The program supported service members, veterans, and their families. When her husband was elected to a second term in 2012, Obama continued to use her time in the White House to help others. In 2014 she created Reach Higher, a program that helped students complete education beyond high school. Then, in 2015, she launched Let Girls Learn with her husband. The program worked to help girls all over the world attend school.

As her husband's second term ended, Obama knew leaving the White House wouldn't be easy. Republican Donald Trump was running for president, and his values didn't match the Obamas'. The Obamas campaigned for Trump's Democratic opponent, Hillary Clinton.

Obama and Hillary Clinton (*left*)

The Obamas welcomed the Trumps to the White House in 2017.

At the 2016 Democratic National Convention, Obama gave a speech. She urged Democrats to stay hopeful and behave as good role models, even as they fought with Republican opponents. "When someone is cruel or acts like a bully, you don't stoop to their level," she said. "No, our motto is, when they go low, we go high."

In 2016 Trump won the presidential election. The Obamas were gracious as they turned over the place they'd called home for eight years to its new occupants.

Obama continued her life's work building community and inspiring others. In November 2018 she published her memoir, *Becoming*, which told the story of her life before, during, and after the White House. The book was a huge success. She toured to talk about it and deliver empowering speeches. In 2019 she was named one of *Time* magazine's one hundred most influential people.

Obama signed copies of *Becoming* on her book tour.

Obama in 2019

Obama's work was never about winning awards or recognition. But the world could see that no matter what she did, she was a powerful woman and a force for change.

GETTING IT DONE

By March 2019, *Becoming* had sold over ten million copies.

TIMELINE

1964   Michelle LaVaughn Robinson is born on January 17. She grows up on the South Side of Chicago.

1985   She graduates from Princeton University.

1992   She marries Barack Obama.

2009   She becomes the United States' first African American First Lady.

2010   She launches her Let's Move! campaign.

2016   She gives her "When They Go Low, We Go High" speech at the Democratic National Convention.

2019   She is named one of *Time* magazine's one hundred most influential people.

GLOSSARY

ambitious: desiring to be successful

application: a formal written request for something such as admission to a school

associate: a lawyer beginning a career

campaigning: taking part in a series of activities to get someone elected

convention: a gathering of people for a common purpose

elected: selected for a position by receiving the most votes

mentor: to teach or give someone advice or guidance

outreach: seeking people out to bring them information or services

privileged: having more advantages than others have

program: a plan of action to achieve a certain result

SOURCE NOTES

5   Michelle Obama, *Becoming* (New York: Crown, 2018), 271.

8   Obama, 40.

8   Obama, 41.

11   Obama, 58.

12   Obama, 66.

17   Obama, 132.

25   "Michelle Obama: 'When They Go Low, We Go High,'" YouTube video, 1:42, posted by *CNN*, July 25, 2016, https://www.youtube.com/watch?v=mu _hCThhzWU.

LEARN MORE

Barack Obama: *Encyclopaedia Britannica*
https://www.britannica.com/biography/Barack-Obama

Harrison, Vashti. *Little Leaders: Bold Women in Black History*. New York: Little, Brown, 2017.

Kanani, Sheila. *The Extraordinary Life of Michelle Obama*. New York: Puffin, 2018.

Machajewski, Sarah. *Michelle Obama*. New York: PowerKids, 2017.

Michelle Obama: *Encyclopaedia Britannica*
https://www.britannica.com/biography/Michelle-Obama

The Office of Barack and Michelle Obama
https://barackobama.com

Orr, Tamra. *Michelle Obama*. Kennett Square, PA: Purple Toad, 2019.

The White House
https://www.whitehouse.gov/

INDEX

PHOTO ACKNOWLEDGMENTS

Image credits: STAN HONDA/AFP/Getty Images, p. 4; PAUL J. RICHARDS/
AFP/Getty Images, pp. 5, 12; Michael Rougier/The LIFE Picture Collection/
Getty Images, p. 6; Rick Friedman/Corbis Historical/Getty Images,
p. 7; Mark Reinstein/Corbis News/Getty Images, p. 8; Scott Olson/
Getty Images, pp. 10, 26; Whitney M. Young Magnet High School, p. 11;
aimintang/iStock/Getty Images, p. 13; Courtesy of Special Collections
Department, Harvard Law School Library, p. 14; Steve Liss/The LIFE
Images Collection/Getty Images, p. 15; Jim Rogash/WireImage/Getty
Images, p. 16; Anda Chu/Media News Group/The Mercury News/Getty
Images, p. 17; AP Photo/Charles Rex Arbogast, p. 18; Chip Somodevilla/
Getty Images, p. 19; David Lienemann/Getty Images, p. 20; Chuck
Kennedy/MCT/Tribune News Service/Getty Images, p. 21; White House
Photo by Chuck Kennedy, p. 22; JEWEL SAMAD/AFP/Getty Images, p. 23;
Alex Wong/Getty Images, p. 24; JIM WATSON/AFP/Getty Images, p. 25;
Paras Griffin/Getty Images, p. 27. Design elements: kondratya/iStock/
Getty Images; iakievy/DigitalVisionVectors/Getty Images; Tanyasun/
iStock/Getty Images; katflare/iStock/Getty Images; mhatzapa/
Shutterstock.com.

Cover: Ethan Miller/Getty Images.